CENTER STAGE

LIONEL RICHIE

By
Teresa Koenig

Edited By
Dr. Howard Schroeder
Professor in Reading and Language Arts
Dept. of Elementary Education
Mankato State University

Produced & Designed By
Baker Street Productions, Ltd.

CRESTWOOD HOUSE

Mankato, Minnesota
U.S.A.

Allen County Public Library
Ft. Wayne, Indiana

LIBRARY OF CONGRESS CATALOGING IN PUBLICATION DATA

Koenig, Teresa.
  Lionel Richie.

  (Center stage)
  Discography: p.
  SUMMARY: Examines the life of the Alabama musician and songwriter who gained
prominence with the Commodores and went on to a highly successful solo career.
  1. Richie, Lionel—Juvenile literature. 2. Rock musicians—United States—Biography—
Juvenile Literature. [1. Richie, Lionel. 2. Musicians. 3. Afro-Americans—Biography.
4. Rock music] I. Schroeder, Howard. II. Title. III. Series.
ML3930.R53K6   1986   784.5'5'00924 [B]   86-13588
ISBN 0-89686-302-6

International Standard
Book Number:
0-89686-302-6

Library of Congress
Catalog Card Number:
86-13588

ILLUSTRATION CREDITS:

Cover: Paul Natkin/Star File
Gary Gershoff/Retna: 4
Nick Elgar/LGI: 7
Lynn Goldsmith/LGI: 9, 12
UPI/Bettmann Newsphotos: 11, 21
Motown: 14
AP/Wide World Photos: 17, 22-23, 26, 28
Leslie Fratkin/LGI: 18
Larry Busacca/Retna: 25
Henry Diltz/USA For Africa: 30

CRESTWOOD HOUSE

Hwy. 66 South, Box 3427
Mankato, MN 56002-3427
507-388-1616

TABLE
OF
CONTENTS

Lionel Richie is one of today's best songwriters and performers.

INTRODUCTION

Too short, too slow, too small

Lionel Richie has proved that nice guys finish first. He is known as one of the best songwriters and performers in the music business. But his success did not come overnight. The success Lionel enjoys today is the result of more than fifteen years of hard work.

In those years, his record albums have been sold to millions of fans around the world. His music has also won awards. Five Grammy Awards, six American Music Awards, and an Oscar from the film industry are just a few of the awards his talent has earned. But Lionel Richie has one special award no one else has been able to top. Every year since 1978, he has had a song become the No. 1 favorite in the country. Only the Beatles, the Rolling Stones, and Stevie Wonder have come close to Lionel's record.

His success goes beyond record sales and awards. Lionel Richie's generosity and concern for people who need help set him apart from many rock stars. "I genuinely like people, that's the first order of business," Lionel explains. "I don't believe that in this world, there's a guy who is too nice." Caring and being nice come naturally for him.

Lionel Richie is at the top of the music world. But when he looks around, he wonders what everyone is so excited about. Reporters and fans "say all these great things about me," he says, "but as far as I'm concerned, I'm still the guy who was too short to play basketball, too slow to run track, and too small to play football."

Luckily for us, Lionel turned his talents to music and finished first.

CHAPTER ONE

An Alabama beginning

Lionel B. Richie, Jr. was born in Tuskegee, Alabama on June 20, 1949. The small southern town had a lot to do with Lionel Richie's success. It is where, in 1881, the former slave, Booker T. Washington, established the first Black college called the Tuskegee Institute.

Learning was always an important goal for the Richie family. Lionel's grandfather had worked in the Tuskegee Institute's business office during the days of Booker T. Washington. And the famous educator's standards were passed on to Lionel. He said, "My goals were those Booker T. Washington set down: good hard work, a sound education, and you do the best you possibly can do."

Lionel was surrounded by teachers while growing up. He lived in a house right across the street from the college. His mother was an elementary school teacher, and later, a high school principal. Lionel never went to school without his homework done. He remembers, "I couldn't get away from homework." His father,

Lionel B. Richie, Sr., a captain in the Army, often helped his son with his studies.

It was Lionel's grandmother, Adelaide Foster, who first taught him about music. She lived nearby and gave piano lessons to several students, including Lionel. The classical composers, Bach and Beethoven, were her favorites. She tried very hard to teach Lionel how to play their music. But, he was not a willing student. ''During my lessons, I kept trying to make up my own songs,'' he recalled. Finally, his grandmother gave up trying to teach him anything about classical music.

He stopped taking lessons, but luckily, he didn't stop making up his own songs.

Lionel poses for a 1984 picture with (left to right) his grandmother, his wife, and his mother.

7

Introducing the Commodores

When it came time for Lionel to choose a college, the decision was easy. He walked across the street and enrolled at the Tuskegee Institute. Lionel's college courses pointed him in a business direction, but he still enjoyed playing music. His Uncle Bertram was a professional musician. He introduced his nephew to the saxophone. But learning how to play it was a struggle.

One day, a classmate of Lionel's, Thomas McClary, spotted him carrying his saxophone across the school campus. He thought Lionel was a musician. McClary stopped him and asked if he'd be interested in joining a band. A campus talent show was coming up and the band needed a saxophone player. The band was called the Jays.

Later Lionel confessed, "What they didn't know, was that I'd brought the horn to school to learn how to play it." At their first rehearsal together, Lionel managed to play his sax well enough to keep his new job. He didn't know it yet, but his future in the music business had just started.

Shortly after Lionel joined the Jays, the bandmembers decided they needed a new name. The six young Tuskegee college freshmen wasted no time finding one. One of them opened a dictionary and took a wild stab at the page. His finger hit the word *Commodore*. They took

The Commodores in a 1981 photo.

a vote, and the Commodores were on their way!

All six Commodores studied for a variety of careers. But what they all had in common was a lot of musical talent and ambition. They had a simple goal. They wanted to be a very successful band.

Drummer, Walter "Clyde" Orange, was the only one in the band who had worked as a professional musician. Milan Williams played keyboards, trombone, and guitar. Ronald LaPread played bass and trumpet.

And William King played several horns while Thomas McClary led on the guitar. Lionel started as the saxophone player, but it wasn't too long before he began singing as well.

The Commodores liked to play a combination of pop and rhythm and blues music. And they soon became known around Tuskegee as a great party band.

At first the Commodores didn't make much money, but they worked hard. By the summer of 1969, they owned their own musical instruments, sound equipment, and costumes. They were ready to look for work outside of Tuskegee. The six singers packed everything into a van and drove to New York City.

A break for the Commodores

Not long after their arrival in New York City, disaster struck. Everything they owned was stolen. Now, how would they find work? Luckily with help, they found out who had their costumes, equipment, and instruments. Unluckily, they had to buy back everything that had been stolen from them.

Finding a job was their only goal, and it didn't take them long to get one. They started appearing nightly at Small's Paradise Club in Harlem, a neighborhood in New York City.

It was at the Paradise Club that Benny Ashton first

saw them perform. Ashton was a local businessman. He thought it would be a good idea to manage a young, talented band. The Commodores met his qualifications. Benny Ashton became their manager before the summer had ended.

Benny Ashton had grown up in the same neighborhood as Suzanne dePasse. Benny and Suzanne had a lot in common. They both managed music groups. Suzanne was the road manager of a new Motown Records group called the Jackson Five. The five brothers attracted a lot of attention with their upbeat love songs. Their lead singer, Michael Jackson, was not even a teenager when they first started out.

Michael Jackson and Lionel first performed on the same stage during a 1971 tour. Here, they accept an award for their song, We Are The World, *in 1986.*

11

In 1971, the Jacksons were getting ready for a concert tour. Suzanne knew they needed a band to open their show. She complained to Benny one day, ''You know I have a problem—I have the Jackson Five and I'm looking for a front act to go out on the road with them on their first U.S. tour.'' Benny hardly let her finish her sentence. He quickly said, ''Look no further, they're in my apartment.''

Suzanne signed the Commodores as the opening act for the Jackson Five. They traveled throughout the United States. By the time the tour ended, the Commodores had their own recording and performing contract with Motown Records.

The Commodores got their first recording contract with Motown in 1971.

CHAPTER TWO

Playing by ear

By the early 1970's, Lionel had improved his playing and singing. But he wanted to do more. All the Commodores' music was being written by the other bandmembers. Lionel made songwriting his next goal.

Being a part of Motown Records meant being part of a family. Lionel now had the chance to learn from many of the most talented songwriters and performers in the music business. At Motown, "Everything was very personal," Diana Ross remembered. "Walking into Motown was like walking into a corner store where you know everybody." Lionel felt at home and got busy finding the right teachers.

Lionel found he could write songs, but he had a problem. Lionel did not read music. That meant he could not write down any musical notes when he composed songs. Instead, Lionel "played by ear." He would hear a melody in his head. On a piano, he picked out the notes that sounded like the melody he heard.

Norman Whitfield, Motown's veteran songwriter, wrote music the same way—by ear. When Lionel found that out, he went to him for advice. One day, he

An early Motown photo of Lionel.

cornered Whitfield and proudly announced, ''I've written a song!'' Norman wanted to hear it right then. But Lionel had recorded the song on an audio cassette. He wanted Norman to wait while he ran and got his tape recorder.

Norman stopped Lionel and said, ''If you've got a great song, hum it to me. No drums, nothing. Lionel, it has to come from the melody.'' It was probably the best piece of advice Lionel ever got about how to write a great song. From then on, every song he wrote had to pass the test of ''the hum.'' He said, ''A great song is one that you can just hum. I try to get my songs to pass that test.''

Gold turns to platinum

Lionel and the Commodores spent much of their time traveling and performing. But they always kept their homebase in Tuskegee. Any time they had off was spent there, resting and planning what they wanted to do next.

The excitement of touring with the Jackson Five, and signing with a major record company, had not made Lionel forget one of his earliest goals. He was determined to finish his education. In 1974, he graduated from the Tuskegee Institute with a degree in economics. By now, he was a fine musician and songwriter. With his college degree, he was better prepared to understand the business side of music.

Business was very good for the Commodores in 1974. They recorded their first album for Motown Records called *Machine Gun*. The title song, *Machine Gun,* was also released as a single record. Music critics liked the song and fans quickly bought over 500,000 copies. When a ''single'' sells that many copies, the artists are given a framed gold copy of their record. The Commodores had their first album and their first gold record.

The Commodores became more popular. They toured regularly and recorded more albums. After the success of *Machine Gun,* they released *Caught In The Act* (1975), *Movin' On* (1975), and *Hit On The Tracks* (1976). But it wasn't until their fifth album, simply called *Commodores*, that a song Lionel wrote became a very big hit. His song, *Easy,* helped give the Commodores their first platinum album. It sold over one million copies.

By 1978, Lionel was the main songwriter for the group. He followed up the success of *Easy* with three more romantic ballads: *Still, Sail On,* and *Three Times A Lady.* Lionel had learned his lessons well. He was easily one of the best ballad writers in the music business.

Thank you
Mrs. Richie

Lionel had written the love song, *Three Times A Lady*, as a "thank you" to his wife, Brenda. They had met in college and married the year after Lionel graduated. When he was not recording albums or touring the country, Brenda made sure Lionel's life at home was happy and stable. He realized that he'd never really told his wife "thank you." His tender love song was one way of letting her know how much he loved and needed her.

The song, Three Times A Lady, *was written for Lionel's wife, Brenda.*

Brenda tries to make Lionel's life at home happy and stable.

In 1980, Brenda helped her husband make one of the most important decisions of his career. Country singer, Kenny Rogers, asked Lionel to write a song for him. Lionel had only written songs for the Commodores and he was worried. He wondered whether he could write for a singer he had never met and didn't know. Besides, Kenny Rogers sang country songs and Lionel didn't. Also, how could he find the time to write? He was about to start a long concert tour with the Commodores. He needed help.

"I selected *Lady* for Kenny," Brenda recalls. "Lionel had written that song about four years earlier. Kenny asked for a song like Lionel's hit ballad, *Three Times A Lady*, and I remembered Lionel had *Lady*. He had only written the first verse of it—that's the way he writes all his songs. He never completes them until he's ready to use them in a project."

Lionel got the two weeks he needed to finish the song, when the Commodores' drummer, "Clyde" Orange, broke his leg in an accident. Everyone went home for a few weeks, except Lionel. He flew to Las Vegas, Nevada to meet with Rogers. Rogers liked Lionel's song and the two men became very good friends.

Brenda was right about *Lady*. It was perfect for Rogers. It proved to be one of Kenny's biggest hit songs. *Lady* was perfect for Lionel, too. He now had proved he could write hit songs for the Commodores and anyone else.

CHAPTER THREE

Duet with Diana

The summer of 1981, was a busy one for Lionel. He and the Commodores were in Los Angeles recording their eleventh album, *In The Pocket*. When Lionel wasn't in the recording studio himself, he was busy across town with Kenny Rogers. Kenny had liked working with Lionel on his single record, *Lady*. He asked Lionel to produce his next album, *Share Your Love*. Not only was Lionel producing the album for Kenny, but he had also written four of the songs.

In the middle of all this, the phone rang one day. As Lionel remembers, "It started out very simply. I received a phone call from the producers of a movie. They asked me to come by and view it. Of course, I had a lot to do and didn't really have the time." Lionel went anyway. He liked the movie and decided to take on another project. The producers wanted him to do what he did best—to write a love song for the film.

The song he wrote was called *Endless Love*, and Diana Ross was to sing it. The producers wanted a male singer to sing the song with Diana. They asked Lionel to suggest someone. He couldn't resist the chance to sing with Diana Ross, so suggested that he do it.

Lionel left Kenny Rogers' recording session in Los Angeles at midnight. He took a plane to Reno, Nevada. They started work at 3:00 a.m. Six hours later, they were done. "It was all very beautiful," Lionel remembers. "It was like magic!"

In 1982, Stevie Wonder got an American Music Award for "Favorite Male Vocalist," and Lionel Richie's song, Endless Love, *won for "Favorite Single."*

A difficult decision

Endless Love was No. 1 on the pop charts for nine weeks. *Endless Love* was another gold record. Lionel

Leaving the Commodores was a hard decision for Lionel to make.

now had the best of both worlds. He worked and toured with his buddies in the Commodores, and had the chance to write, perform, and produce records with other talented artists.

In 1982, Lionel announced his plans to make an album of his own, without the Commodores. Music critics and reporters began asking him if he wanted to leave the Commodores and go out on his own? He didn't want to think about leaving the band. He had been with them almost fifteen years. They were his long-time friends.

The more music projects he took on alone, the more he realized how much he liked solo work. "I have a feeling of freedom and individuality," Lionel told a reporter. "I like that feeling and I don't really have it as much with the Commodores." His strengths were in writing and singing soft love songs. Lionel began to see that his musical talents and tastes were growing away from the Commodores' rhythm and blues style.

Lionel's decision to finally leave the band was not easy. "We had spent fifteen years together," he said. "Not to perform with them on tour and on record was the most difficult decision I've ever had to make."

It had been a good fifteen years for the Commodores. They had recorded four gold and three platinum albums. Lionel and the Commodores would always be friends.

Singing solo

One of the toughest decisions a gifted artist has to make is to leave the safety of his or her group or band. Lionel took the risk and started performing on his own.

Once on his own, he didn't regret his decision.

His first solo album was called *Lionel Richie.* One of the songs on the album, *Truly,* won him his first Grammy Award. After winning one of the music industry's highest honors, he prepared for his first concert tour without the Commodores. By the fall of 1983, he was ready to step out on stage alone.

He opened his tour to a sold out crowd in Toledo, Ohio. Sold out in Toledo meant ten thousand people had paid to see Lionel Richie. He was nervous and

By 1983, Lionel was singing on stage alone.

Melissa Manchester presents Lionel with his first Grammy in 1983.

worried that he might disappoint his fans. He didn't have to worry long. After the first song, the crowd cheered, clapped, and stood up to welcome him. Lionel couldn't believe it. He remembered how good he felt at that moment, ''I felt I was home, back again, and it was wonderful!''

Can't slow down

Lionel's second solo album, *Can't Slow Down,* was an even bigger success than his first. It quickly became the biggest selling record in the history of Motown

Records. Five songs from the album became hit singles: *All Night Long, Penny Lover, Hello, Running With The Night,* and *Stuck On You.* Within the year, he won two more Grammy Awards and picked up six American Music Awards for his latest recording effort.

Another, even bigger, concert tour was organized for the summer of 1984. ''Playing live is just the best,'' Lionel admitted. ''One of the most gratifying things about being a songwriter and performer is going on the road and running into people whose lives my songs have touched. I share my life with the whole world through my songs. This is especially true on stage. I love being out there.''

His fans were never disappointed. Alone at the piano, he began each show with his first Grammy award-winning song, *Truly.* Then the seven-piece band behind Lionel broke into the song, *Serves You Right.* Lionel just kept on playing his hits, one by one—*Sail On, Easy, Penny Lover, Hello,* and many more.

A party broke out on stage as he went into his last number, *All Night Long.* Dancers joined him on stage and fireworks burst overhead. For his fans, ''all night long'' was how long he could have sung for them!

An Olympic-size party

On a warm August evening in Los Angeles, California, Lionel sang a special twenty minute version of *All*

Night Long. The 1984 Summer Olympic Games had just ended. Lionel had been chosen to sing at the closing celebration. There wasn't an empty seat in the Los Angeles Coliseum that night.

Gathered down on the field were two hundred break dancers and several thousand Olympic athletes and volunteer staff people. Fireworks exploded and a spaceship model appeared overhead. It was one of the biggest parties of all time.

Everyone on the field danced to Lionel's dazzling salute. While Olympic athletes moved around Lionel's center stage, almost 2.5 billion people watched it all on television. He sang to the world that night. "We need to forget our differences and dance together and celebrate our dreams," Lionel explained. "The Olympic Games show how very much we have in common."

Lionel sang to the world at the close of the 1984 Summer Olympic Games.

CHAPTER FOUR

We Are The World

Lionel believed in celebrating dreams. And he did more than sing about it. He had always had strong feelings about education. For the past few years, he had been giving his time and money to set up special educational programs. He wanted to help kids stay in school.

But there were other issues that were important to him. In Africa millions of people were dying and needed help. In early January, 1985, Lionel was asked to head-up the U.S.A. for Africa (*United Support of Artists for Africa*) project. A song had to be written for a special recording session. The money earned from its record sales would go to buy food, medicine, and equipment for the people of Africa. He called on an old friend, Michael Jackson, for help. In little more than a week they wrote the song, *We Are The World*.

A party for life

On January 28, 1985, Lionel's hard work for U.S.A. for Africa paid off. In a West Hollywood recording studio, he had gathered over forty of America's top pop and rock stars. Bruce Springsteen, Willie Nelson, Tina Turner, Michael Jackson, Stevie Wonder and many more came that night to make an important record. They had only one night to rehearse and record the song. Quincy Jones, the conductor, started the session at 10:00 p.m. and kept everyone working through the night.

Lionel noticed how easily everyone in the room worked together. "We stopped being powerful as individuals and became a unit," he noted. It was

Lionel gathered over forty of America's top musicians to record We Are The World.

morning when Springsteen finished the last solo. Bruce gave Lionel his autograph and left. The session was over.

Lionel looked back over the evening and said, "There's no greater gift than the gift of life. That's what we realized by being here. It was a party for life."

He was right. The album, *We Are The World,* raised almost fifty million dollars (US) for Africa in one year. The success of the effort set an example for several other fund raising events. The Live Aid concert in July, 1985, and the Farm Aid concert in September, 1985, were organized for the same reason—to save lives.

Movie music

Later in 1985, another challenge came Lionel's way. Film director Taylor Hackford, wanted him to write a title song for his movie, *White Nights.* The title song is very important. "I wanted a title song that would show the message of this film," explained Hackford, "the need to count on your friends and . . . freedom, which can only be achieved through cooperation and love."

Lionel and his manager, Ken Kragen, watched the movie in a private screening room. Lionel understood what type of song the director needed. He went right to work on it.

The song was called *Say You, Say Me.* Released in

the fall of 1985, it swiftly climbed to No. 1 on the pop charts. And on March 24, 1986, *Say You, Say Me* won an Oscar. As the Grammy award is to the record business, so the Oscar is to the film industry. Composers and musicians who write and play music for films voted *Say You, Say Me* the Best Song of the Year.

Seated with his wife and mother at the awards ceremony, Lionel looked stunned when they announced his name. It took a few seconds for everything to sink in. He carefully climbed the steps to the stage. As one billion people around the world watched on television, Lionel thanked everyone. Then, holding his Oscar high in the air, an excited Lionel said, "This is outrageous!"

Lionel plans ahead

"Too much is not enough—that's my motto," says Lionel with a smile on his face. He says this casually, but he couldn't be more serious. Working or playing, Lionel gives one hundred per cent of his energy. "I like a lot of things going on at once. I like waking up in the morning and feeling like I'm on the edge of a cliff—that there is a new challenge." Being on the edge for Lionel is doing things people don't expect him to do.

Lionel Richie has a lot planned for his future. There will no doubt be more albums and tours. He also dreams about acting in movies. It's unlikely he'll ever slow down. He doesn't know how.